Michel Cii

A Biography of the Critic Who Shaped Cinema's Heart. His Life, Passion, Prose, and Enduring Legacy

Olivia Gates

Dedicated to the future

Table of Contents

Acknowledgement

A big thank you to my family and friends. I love you all

Introduction: A Champion of Cinema - The Life and Legacy of Michel Ciment

Michel Ciment wasn't just a film critic; he was a flame-bearer, a torch illuminating the intricacies and profound depths of cinema for generations. Born in Paris in 1938, Ciment's life became an inseparable thread woven into the fabric of cinematic history. This biography aims to unravel the tapestry of his journey, exploring not just his personal trajectory but also the indelible mark he left on the landscape of film criticism.

Background and Early Life:

Ciment's formative years were steeped in the intellectual milieu of post-war Paris. The son of Polish immigrants, he found solace and inspiration in the darkened halls of cinemas, devouring films with the insatiable curiosity of a budding cinephile. He honed his analytical prowess amidst the vibrant discussions at the Cinémathèque française, his peers becoming lifelong collaborators and companions. This fertile ground nourished his passion, leading him to the doorstep of the legendary film magazine Positif, where he found not just a platform, but a pulpit.

Overview of Ciment's Impact on Film Criticism:

Ciment's arrival at Positif marked a turning point in the magazine's history. His infectious enthusiasm, coupled with his meticulous scholarship, breathed new life into the publication. He championed American cinema, then often dismissed by European critics, recognizing its artistic merit and cultural significance. His unwavering advocacy helped bridge the transatlantic divide, fostering a dialogue that enriched both cinematic traditions.

But Ciment's influence transcended individual pieces and publications. He championed a critical approach that treated cinema as art, demanding rigorous analysis and intellectual engagement. He believed in the power of film to not just entertain but to illuminate the human condition, explore social complexities, and provoke introspection. His writings, laced with insightful observations and nuanced arguments, inspired generations of critics and cinephiles to approach cinema with the same reverence and respect.

This biography delves deeper into the man behind the words, exploring the personal convictions that shaped his critical lens. It examines the intellectual currents that informed his analyses, the filmmakers he championed, and the controversies he navigated. Importantly, it also investigates the legacy he leaves behind, the imprint he left on the world of film criticism, and the enduring flame of passion he ignited in countless cinephiles around the globe.

So, turn the page, dear reader, and let us embark on this journey into the life and legacy of Michel Ciment, a man who dedicated his life to deciphering the magic of cinema and sharing its wonders with the world.

Chapter One: The Early Years

Michel Ciment was born in Paris in 1938, a city still bearing the scars of a world recently ravaged by war. Yet, amidst the shadows of conflict, flickered a tiny ember of resilience: the cinema. This haven of light and celluloid would become Ciment's sanctuary, the crucible in which his life's passion would be forged.

Childhood and Family Influences:

The Ciment household was a haven of intellectual discourse, fueled by the stories his Polish immigrant parents brought with them. His father, a tailor by trade, possessed a keen intellect and a deep love for literature, particularly the works of Dostoevsky and Tolstoy. This fascination with the complexities of human nature and the moral ambiguity of existence would deeply influence Ciment's future outlook on cinema. His mother, imbued with a spirit of resilience and a vibrant curiosity for the world, instilled in him an insatiable appetite for exploration and discovery.

However, it was his older brother, André, who ignited Ciment's initial spark of cinematic passion. André, an avid cinephile, introduced Michel to the wonders of flickering images and captivating narratives. Weekends were spent huddled in darkened theatres, devouring American gangster films, Italian neorealism masterpieces, and the poignant poetry of French New Wave auteurs. André's infectious enthusiasm laid the foundation for Ciment's lifelong devotion to cinema, becoming his guide and confidante in this nascent obsession.

Early Exposure to Cinema:

Paris in the 1940s and 50s was a burgeoning cinephile Mecca. The Cinémathèque Française, a temple dedicated to the cinematic archive, became Ciment's second home. Surrounded by fellow devotees, he delved into the silent era's silent poetry, marveled at the grandeur of Hollywood musicals, and dissected the intricacies of European art films. The Cinémathèque's diverse offerings provided a cinematic banquet, nourishing Ciment's burgeoning critical faculties and challenging him to dissect the language of film with increasing analytical acuity.

One film, in particular, left an indelible mark: Jean Renoir's "La Règle du Jeu" (The Rules of the Game). Its witty dialogue, layered narrative, and poignant portrayal of human foibles ignited a profound understanding of cinema's potential to dissect the human experience. It wasn't just entertainment; it was a mirror reflecting the complexities of life, a canvas upon which emotions were rendered in light and shadow. This epiphany cemented Ciment's path: he wouldn't just love cinema; he would dedicate his life to understanding and explaining its profound power.

The early years, though shadowed by a war-torn world, laid the foundation for Ciment's extraordinary journey. The intellectual richness of his family, the shared passion with his brother, and the immersive experience of the Cinémathèque ignited a fire within him. This chapter paints a portrait of a young cinephile in the making, his love for film blossoming amidst the bustling cultural milieu of post-war Paris. It sets the stage for the next chapter, where his passion would find its voice and begin to influence the world around him.

Chapter Two: Education and Entry into Film Criticism

Michel Ciment's cinematic apprenticeship didn't end within the dimly lit halls of the Cinémathèque. The intellectual rigor of academia provided another crucial crucible, shaping his analytical prowess and honing his critical voice. While film schools were yet to rise in prominence, Ciment navigated the labyrinthine corridors of Parisian education, acquiring a diverse set of skills that would later prove invaluable in his exploration of the cinematic landscape.

Academic Background:

Driven by a thirst for knowledge that extended beyond the silver screen, Ciment enrolled at the prestigious Lycée Louis-le-Grand. Steeped in classical studies and French literature, the school nurtured his linguistic talents and instilled in him meticulous attention to detail. These skills would become instrumental in his future analyses, allowing him to dissect film narratives with the precision of a surgeon and deconstruct their underlying thematic complexities.

While literature remained a cornerstone of his education, history beckoned as well. Immersed in the turbulent narrative of France's past, Ciment developed a keen understanding of social and political currents, a lens that would later prove invaluable in deciphering the cultural and historical contexts of films. Studying figures like Sartre and Foucault further refined his critical thinking, sharpening his ability to analyze power structures and ideological frameworks as they played out on screen.

However, the pull of cinema never truly faded. Throughout his academic years, Ciment continued to devour films, his appetite whetted by the Cinémathèque and fueled by burgeoning discussions with like-minded individuals. He discovered the Cahiers du cinéma, a vibrant magazine buzzing with the intellectual fervor of the New Wave. Its passionate critiques and audacious pronouncements resonated deeply with Ciment, further solidifying his desire to join the ranks of those dissecting the art form he loved.

Initial Interest in Film:

While film remained his core passion, Ciment's academic explorations yielded unexpected synergies. His linguistic training enabled him to appreciate the subtleties of dialogue and the evocative power of language in film. Historical studies sharpened his awareness of cinema's ability to reflect and refract societal shifts. Literature provided him with an arsenal of analytical tools, allowing him to dissect narrative structures and uncover the thematic depths hidden within celluloid narratives.

This interdisciplinary tapestry fueled Ciment's burgeoning desire to engage critically with cinema. He began scribbling reviews, honing his voice through clandestine publications circulated amongst fellow cinephiles. These early forays were more than just exercises in critique; they were acts of self-discovery, allowing him to test his analytical muscles and articulate his burgeoning passion for film in a structured format.

Joining the World of Film Criticism:

Fate, much like a well-timed plot twist, intervened in 1963. An auspicious encounter with François Truffaut, then editor of Positif magazine, opened a door that seemed almost preordained. Ciment's audacious defense of Orson Welles, published in the magazine, caught Truffaut's eye. Impressed by his intellectual rigor and refreshingly unorthodox views, Truffaut offered him a position at Positif.

Positif, in its post-war heyday, was a bustling hub of critical discourse. Its contributors, a pantheon of cinephiles like Jean-Luc Godard and Jacques Rivette, had redefined film criticism as a vibrant intellectual pursuit. Joining their ranks was no small feat; it was a baptism by fire, a demanding proving ground where one's ideas were dissected and debated with fierce passion.

Yet, Ciment thrived in this crucible of critical ferment. He embraced the intellectual sparring, his arguments sharpened by rigorous debates and his perspective enriched by diverse viewpoints. His writing, fueled by his academic background and cinematic passion, gained a distinctive voice – a blend of scholarly insight, unwavering conviction, and an infectious enthusiasm for cinema's endless possibilities.

Ciment's early years at Positif were marked by audacious pronouncements and unwavering championing of American cinema. He challenged the Eurocentric bias prevalent in French criticism, recognizing the artistic merit and cultural significance of Hollywood Westerns, gangster films, and the works of American auteurs like John Ford and Howard Hawks.

His defense of American cinema went beyond mere cultural exchange; it was a recognition of film's universal language, and its ability to transcend borders and speak to the human condition in all its complexity. This perspective resonated with a new generation of cinephiles, eager to expand their horizons and explore the diverse offerings of international cinema.

Beyond championing American cinema, Ciment embraced the eclectic richness of the cinematic landscape. He championed European art films, dissected the burgeoning New Wave movements, and delved into the social realism of Italian cinema. His articles, ranging from passionate defenses of underappreciated gems to insightful analyses of cinematic giants, established him as a leading voice in the critical vanguard.

Ciment's entry into film criticism wasn't a mere happenstance; it was a culmination of his lifelong passion, fueled by academic rigor, intellectual debates,

Chapter Three: Positif Magazine and Film Criticism Career

Positif became Michel Ciment's canvas, and his words danced across its pages, shaping not only his own career but also the landscape of French film criticism. Here, amongst the passionate debates and intellectual fervor, Ciment's voice rose, distinct and powerful, leaving an indelible mark on the magazine and the world of cinema.

Role at "Positif" Magazine:

Ciment's arrival at Positif was not just a personal victory; it marked a turning point for the magazine itself. His infectious enthusiasm, coupled with his scholarly expertise, breathed new life into the publication. He championed a critical approach that treated cinema as art, demanding rigorous analysis and intellectual engagement. He believed in the power of film to not just entertain but to illuminate the human condition, explore social complexities, and provoke introspection.

His writing reflected this philosophy. His reviews were more than mere critiques; they were insightful essays, dissecting narratives, unpacking symbolism, and drawing comparisons across cinematic landscapes. He tackled American directors like Altman and Scorsese with the same meticulous attention as he analyzed European auteurs like Bresson and Kiarostami. His work transcended national boundaries, establishing him as a champion of global cinema.

Beyond writing, Ciment became a driving force behind Positif's evolution. He pushed the magazine to engage with emerging trends, championing independent cinema and exploring genres often dismissed by mainstream critics. He fostered collaborations with international film publications, opening dialogues and bridging cultural gaps. Under his influence, Positif became more than a magazine; it became a critical platform, a sounding board for diverse voices, and a vibrant forum for cinephiles across the globe.

Evolution of Film Criticism in France:

Ciment's contributions were not solely confined to Positif. He actively participated in shaping the broader landscape of French film criticism. He became a vocal advocate for a pluralistic approach, challenging the elitist tendencies that had long dominated the scene. He argued for a critical practice that engaged with popular cinema, acknowledged genre films' artistic merit, and embraced the diverse experiences of different audiences.

He challenged the rigid auteur theory that had dominated French criticism, arguing for a more nuanced understanding of cinematic authorship. He recognized the collaborative nature of filmmaking, the influence of social and historical contexts, and the importance of audience reception in shaping the meaning of a film.

Ciment's emphasis on the social and political dimensions of cinema further fueled this evolution. He saw the film as a reflection of our times, a mirror reflecting societal anxieties, power structures, and ideological struggles. His analyses delved into the hidden messages and subtle subtexts, urging viewers to become active participants in the critical process, not passive consumers of images.

This critical approach resonated with a new generation of cinephiles disillusioned with the elitism of traditional film criticism. Ciment's work became a bridge between the intellectual rigor of the old guard and the accessibility craved by the new. He made film criticism relevant, engaging, and accessible to a broader audience, democratizing the critical discourse and sparking a renewed passion for the art form.

Influential Works and Reviews:

Ciment's contributions to film criticism are vast and multifaceted. His book-length analyses of directors like Alfred Hitchcock, John Ford, and Akira Kurosawa remain indispensable resources for scholars and cinephiles alike. His essay collection,

"Hitchcock", published in 1960, revolutionized the understanding of the master of suspense, shedding light on the psychological depths and narrative complexities of his films.

His reviews, scattered across the pages of Positif and other publications, stand as a testament to his critical mastery. They are not mere pronouncements of judgment; they are miniature narratives, weaving together insightful observations, historical context, and personal reflections to create a tapestry of understanding around each film.

His review of Sergio Leone's "Once Upon a Time in the West", for instance, went beyond the traditional Western tropes to unveil a meditation on mortality, memory, and the myths of the American frontier. Similarly, his analysis of Michael Haneke's "Cache" unearthed the film's anxieties about surveillance, guilt, and the fragility of personal narratives.

These are just a few examples of Ciment's influential works. Each review, each essay, each book bore the hallmark of his critical acumen – his meticulous attention to detail, his unwavering passion for cinema, and his ability to illuminate the profound depths hidden within the flickering images on screen.

Ciment's legacy extends beyond individual works. He fostered a generation of film critics, inspiring them with his rigorous approach, his intellectual honesty, and his unwavering belief in the power of cinema. He created a critical space where diverse voices could be heard, where films could be dissected with rigor and passion, and where the love for cinema could be celebrated freely.

In this chapter, we have explored Michel Ciment's pivotal role at Positif magazine, his contribution to the evolution of French film criticism,

Chapter Four: Ciment's Approach to Film Analysis - Unraveling the Magic on the Screen

Michel Ciment wasn't just a film critic; he was a cartographer, meticulously charting the intricate landscapes of cinema with a unique critical compass. His analysis wasn't a mere dissection of technical elements or a rote application of theoretical frameworks; it was a vibrant dance between intellect, passion, and historical context, a quest to illuminate the magic flickering on the screen. This chapter delves into the philosophical and theoretical foundations that shaped Ciment's inimitable approach to film analysis.

Philosophical and Theoretical Influences:

Ciment's intellectual wellspring wasn't confined to the darkened halls of cinemas or the pages of film magazines. He drew inspiration from a diverse array of philosophical and theoretical currents, forging a tapestry of critical insights that enriched his engagement with cinema.

His early readings of Sartre and Foucault instilled in him a keen awareness of power structures and ideological frameworks, providing him with tools to dissect the social and political dimensions of films. He saw cinema as a reflection of our times, a vessel carrying anxieties, prejudices, and the shifting sands of historical landscapes. His analyses, therefore, weren't just evaluations of aesthetics; they were explorations of the cultural and political subtexts embedded within narratives and visuals.

The psychoanalytic theories of Freud and Lacan further informed his methodology. He delved into the psychological depths of characters, unraveling the hidden complexities of human motivations and desires. He recognized the power of the subconscious, the interplay between dreams and reality, and the ways in which cinema could tap into the primordial fears and anxieties lurking within the human psyche.

Beyond these traditional frameworks, Ciment embraced the evolving landscape of critical theory. He engaged with semiotics, recognizing the symbolic language of film and the layered meanings encoded within every frame. He delved into genre studies, appreciating the power of generic conventions and the ways in which filmmakers subvert, manipulate, or play with established tropes.

However, Ciment wasn't a slave to theory. He never allowed theoretical frameworks to constrain his critical voice or stifle his intuitive response to the films themselves. He used theory as a lens, not a bludgeon, a tool to enhance his understanding, not a rigid script to dictate his analyses.

Methodology in Film Analysis:

Ciment's approach to film analysis was as multifaceted as the cinematic landscapes he traversed. He refused to be confined to a single methodology, instead employing a flexible toolkit that embraced both rigor and intuition.

His analyses often began with a meticulous attention to detail. He dissects visuals, analyzing camera movements, framing, and the mise-en-scène. He delves into the intricacies of sound design, music, and dialogue, recognizing their influence in shaping mood, atmosphere, and narrative progression. He unpacks the symbolism embedded within costumes, props, and even the physical landscapes within the film.

Yet, Ciment's analysis wasn't confined to surface elements. He delved into the narrative structures, tracing the threads of plot, exploring their thematic implications, and uncovering the deeper meanings woven into the narrative tapestry. He examines the character arcs, grappling with motivations, desires, and the complex moral landscapes they navigate.

Furthermore, Ciment never analyzed films in isolation. He recognized the importance of historical context, situating films within their cultural and political zeitgeist. He drew comparisons across cinematic landscapes, tracing threads of influence and exploring the evolution of genres and thematic concerns. His analyses were often infused with references to literature, philosophy, and other artistic disciplines, illuminating the intertextual dialogue that enriches the experience of film.

Crucially, Ciment never lost sight of the emotional core of cinema. His analyses pulsated with his own passionate response to the films, acknowledging the visceral impact of images and sounds. He recognized the power of cinema to evoke empathy, challenge perspectives, and ignite critical thought. This personal engagement, this unashamed expression of his own love and awe for cinema, is what truly set Ciment's approach apart.

Ciment's methodology wasn't a formula; it was a conversation, a dynamic interplay between rigorous analysis, historical awareness, personal engagement, and an unwavering fascination with the magic flickering on the screen. He wasn't just dissecting films; he was inviting viewers to join him on a journey of discovery, a shared pursuit of meaning within the ever-expanding universe of cinema.

This chapter has explored the philosophical and theoretical underpinnings of Ciment's approach, and his flexible methodology for unraveling the complexities of film. In the next chapter, we will delve deeper into his relationship with specific filmmakers and how his critical voice shaped the reception and understanding of their work.

Chapter Five: Notable Publications - Beacons in the Cinematic Landscape

Michel Ciment wasn't just a film critic; he was a chronicler, meticulously documenting and illuminating the vast cinematic landscape through his prolific and insightful publications. Beyond his countless reviews and essays scattered across the pages of film magazines, Ciment crafted books that stand as towering monuments, testaments to his dedication to understanding and sharing the magic of cinema.

Authorship of Books on Cinema:

Ciment's books transcended the limitations of traditional critical analyses. They weren't mere collections of reviews stitched together; they were immersive journeys into the minds and worlds of the filmmakers he championed. Each book became a beacon, guiding readers through the intricate complexities of a director's vision, shedding light on their stylistic choices, thematic preoccupations, and the enduring impact of their work.

His book "Hitchcock", published in 1960, revolutionized the understanding of the master of suspense. It delved beyond the superficial thrills and macabre delights, uncovering the psychological depths and narrative complexities that lay beneath the surface. Ciment dissected Hitchcock's use of camera, editing, and symbolism, revealing the meticulous control he exerted over audience perception and fear. This groundbreaking work became an essential reference for scholars and cinephiles alike, forever altering the lens through which we view Hitchcock's cinematic creations.

Similarly, his book "Kubrick" (1980) offered a comprehensive and nuanced portrait of the enigmatic auteur. He tackled Kubrick's diverse filmography, from the bleak satire of "Dr. Strangelove" to the existential anxieties of "2001: A Space Odyssey," with intellectual rigor and passionate appreciation. Ciment explored Kubrick's fascination with technology, his preoccupation with death and mortality, and his relentless pursuit of cinematic perfection. This in-depth analysis became a must-read for anyone seeking to grasp the full depth and brilliance of Kubrick's vision.

Beyond these individual director studies, Ciment's books broadened the scope of cinematic exploration. "Kazan par Kazan" (1973) offered an intimate glimpse into the life and work of Elia Kazan, weaving together interviews and critical analysis to create a multifaceted portrait of the American filmmaker. "Boorman: Un visionnaire en son temps" (1985) championed John Boorman's visionary work, showcasing his thematic richness, genre-bending experiments, and unwavering commitment to social commentary.

Ciment's publications weren't confined to solitary auteurs; he also curated anthologies that ignited dialogues and explored diverse cinematic currents. "Le Dossier Rosi" (1976) delved into the Italian neorealist roots and political concerns of Francesco Rosi. "Passeport pour Hollywood" (1992) brought together insightful interviews with American legends like Billy Wilder, John Huston, and Billy Wilder, offering a firsthand glimpse into their creative processes and perspectives on the Hollywood landscape.

Contribution to Film Scholarship:

Ciment's impact on film scholarship extended far beyond the pages of his own books. His meticulously researched essays, published in renowned journals and anthologies, enriched critical discourse and sparked crucial conversations within the field. His work on American cinema, often neglected by European critics, helped bridge the transatlantic divide, fostering mutual understanding and appreciation.

His engagement with diverse cinematic traditions, from Japanese masters like Kurosawa to Latin American auteurs like Glauber Rocha, broadened the scope of film studies, challenging Eurocentric biases and highlighting the richness and complexity of global cinema. He championed independent filmmakers and under-appreciated gems, bringing them to the attention of a wider audience and influencing the critical discourse surrounding their work.

Ciment's contribution to film scholarship also lies in his unwavering intellectual honesty. He wasn't afraid to engage in critical debate, challenge established interpretations, and revise his perspectives as his understanding of cinema evolved. His willingness to engage in dialogues, acknowledge blind spots, and embrace new avenues of critical inquiry served as a model for aspiring scholars and film enthusiasts alike.

Furthermore, Ciment's books inspired generations of critics, writers, and filmmakers. His meticulous research, insightful analysis, and passionate engagement with cinema set a high bar for critical excellence. He demonstrated that film criticism could be both academically rigorous and engagingly written, fostering a new generation of scholars who approached cinema with the same intellectual curiosity and fervor as Ciment himself.

In conclusion, Michel Ciment's publications didn't just document the cinematic landscape; they actively shaped it. They served as beacons, guiding viewers and scholars through the complexities of filmmakers' visions, enriching the discourse of film studies, and leaving an indelible mark on the world of cinema. His books stand as testaments to his enduring legacy, a testament to his unwavering belief in the power of film to illuminate the human condition and inspire critical thought.

Chapter Six: Navigating the Currents: Controversies and Criticisms

Michel Ciment's journey through the cinematic landscape wasn't without its turbulent waters. His passionate advocacy, his unorthodox perspectives, and his unwavering critical voice inevitably stirred the pot, sparking debates and occasionally attracting criticism. This chapter delves into the controversies and criticisms Ciment faced, navigating the currents of dissent and understanding the motivations behind them.

Reception of Ciment's Critiques:

Ciment's early championing of American cinema in a landscape dominated by Eurocentric biases was bound to ruffle feathers. Critics accused him of cultural imperialism, arguing that he overlooked the brilliance of European auteurs by lionizing Hollywood genre films and westerns. However, Ciment's unwavering appreciation for the artistic merit and cultural significance of American cinema challenged these entrenched biases, paving the way for a more nuanced appreciation of global film.

Even within the realm of American cinema, Ciment wasn't afraid to go against the grain. His defense of John Ford, then often dismissed as a mere genre filmmaker, highlighted the thematic depth and stylistic mastery of his Westerns. Similarly, his championing of Alfred Hitchcock, while widely admired, wasn't universally embraced. Some critics found his psychoanalytic interpretations intrusive, arguing that they overshadowed the filmmaker's artistic vision.

However, Ciment's most contentious critiques often arose from his unflinching honesty and willingness to engage with the shortcomings of even his most admired filmmakers. His criticism of Kubrick's later works, such as "Eyes Wide Shut," for their perceived coldness and cynicism, sparked debate among Kubrick devotees. Similarly, his analysis of Akira Kurosawa's later period, while recognizing his mastery, pointed out a potential thematic repetitiveness, provoking passionate counter-arguments from Kurosawa enthusiasts.

Controversial Perspectives and Debates:

Beyond individual critiques, Ciment's broader perspectives on film criticism itself often ignited controversy. His advocacy for a pluralistic approach, embracing genre films and popular cinema alongside art-house fare, challenged the elitist tendencies that had long dominated the critical landscape. This stance earned him accusations of pandering to mass tastes and sacrificing intellectual rigor for accessibility.

Furthermore, Ciment's championing of directors like Michael Haneke, with their unflinching depictions of human cruelty and existential despair, provoked discomfort among some critics. They argued that his admiration for Haneke's bleak vision amounted to endorsing pessimism and cynicism. Ciment, on the other hand, saw Haneke's films as essential challenges to complacency, forcing viewers to confront the darkness within humanity and the complexities of the modern world.

One of the most enduring debates revolved around Ciment's relationship with auteur theory. While acknowledging its significance in elevating film criticism to a serious academic pursuit, he cautioned against a rigid application of its principles. He argued for a more nuanced understanding of authorship, recognizing the collaborative nature of filmmaking and the influence of historical context on the final product. This sparked passionate arguments among proponents of a strict auteur theory who saw his perspective as a dilution of its core principles.

However, it's crucial to understand that Ciment didn't court controversy intentionally. His dissenting opinions arose from his intellectual honesty, his unwavering passion for cinema in all its diverse forms, and his constant стремление to engage in meaningful dialogue. He embraced challenges, welcomed opposing viewpoints, and used debate as a catalyst for deeper understanding and critical growth.

Ultimately, Ciment's legacy transcends the controversies and criticisms. His willingness to engage in nuanced, intellectually rigorous discourse enriched the world of film criticism. His unwavering enthusiasm for cinema, regardless of its genre or origin, broadened the scope of appreciation and ignited passion in countless cinephiles. He demonstrated that criticism, at its best, isn't a weapon to wield, but a bridge to build, a shared journey to unravel the intricacies of a beloved art form.

Chapter Seven: A Ripple Across the Globe - Michel Ciment's Enduring Impact

Michel Ciment's influence wasn't confined to the pages of film magazines or the Parisian intellectual circles. His passionate voice resonated far beyond national borders, sending ripples across the cinematic landscape, and leaving an indelible mark on both French cinema and international film criticism.

Influence on French Cinema:

Ciment's impact on French cinema began in the crucible of Positif magazine. He injected a newfound energy and intellectual rigor into the publication, fostering a space for diverse voices and championing emerging film trends. His unwavering support for genre films and American cinema challenged the Eurocentric bias prevalent in French criticism, prompting a reevaluation of cinematic merit beyond national origins.

French filmmakers themselves responded to Ciment's championing. The New Wave auteurs, a generation seeking to break free from established cinematic traditions, found an ally in his critical voice. His insightful analyses of their work and unwavering support provided them with crucial validation during their formative years.

Beyond direct support, Ciment's critical framework influenced the trajectory of French cinema. His emphasis on social and political realities resonated with filmmakers like Claire Denis and Claude Lanzmann, prompting them to explore contemporary anxieties and historical complexities within their narratives. His championing of genre films encouraged experimentation and the subversion of traditional tropes, evident in the works of Olivier Assayas and Leos Carax.

Even established French masters recognized the breadth and depth of Ciment's knowledge. He became a trusted confidante and collaborator for figures like Jean-Luc Godard and François Truffaut, engaging in critical dialogues that further enriched their cinematic visions.

Ciment's impact wasn't solely confined to specific filmmakers; he actively shaped the critical discourse surrounding French cinema. His insightful essays and reviews in Positif and other international publications provided audiences and scholars with nuanced perspectives on French films, fostering a deeper understanding and appreciation for their cultural and artistic significance.

He championed neglected figures like Jacques Rozier and Jacques Tourneur, bringing their works to the attention of a wider audience. He challenged established interpretations of classics like Jean Renoir's "La Règle du Jeu," offering fresh insights that illuminated the film's enduring artistic and thematic relevance.

In essence, Ciment became a vital bridge between French cinema and the world. He translated the complexities of French aesthetics and cultural nuances for international audiences, while simultaneously introducing global cinematic currents to French viewers. His work fostered cross-cultural dialogues, enriching both sides of the cinematic equation.

International Recognition:

Beyond France, Ciment's voice reverberated across the global cinematic landscape. His contributions to international film festivals, his participation in critical symposiums, and his tireless advocacy for diverse cinema cemented his stature as a leading figure in international film criticism.

He served on juries at Cannes, Venice, and Berlin, ensuring diverse perspectives and a celebration of cinematic excellence beyond national boundaries. His lectures and workshops at prestigious institutions like New York University and the Cinémathèque Française disseminated his critical insights and inspired students and scholars across the globe.

Ciment's publications transcended national borders, being translated into multiple languages and finding dedicated readerships across continents. His books on Hitchcock, Kubrick, and other auteur figures became staples in university curriculums and private libraries, introducing new generations to the intricacies of film analysis and the enduring magic of cinema.

Furthermore, Ciment actively fostered critical dialogues across countries. He collaborated with renowned international film critics like Roger Ebert and Jonathan Rosenbaum, engaging in insightful debates and challenging established critical approaches. He welcomed diverse perspectives, encouraged the translation of critical works, and actively participated in building a global community of cinephiles united by their passion for film.

In conclusion, Michel Ciment's impact on cinema wasn't confined to a single nation or a specific artistic movement. His voice echoed across continents, shaping film criticism, influencing filmmakers, and inspiring countless cinephiles to engage with the magic of cinema on a deeper level. He leaves behind a legacy of unwavering passion, intellectual rigor, and a love for the art form that transcended borders and languages.

Chapter Eight: Beyond Criticism - Academic and Filmmaking Connections

While Michel Ciment's primary claim to fame lies in his masterful film criticism, his intellectual thirst and creative spirit led him to explore other avenues within the cinematic landscape. This chapter delves into his diverse academic engagements and collaborative ventures with filmmakers, revealing the multifaceted nature of his contribution to the world of cinema.

Academic Engagements:

Beyond the bustling world of film magazines and festivals, Ciment found a second intellectual home in the hallowed halls of academia. He actively participated in conferences and symposiums, engaging in rigorous debates on film theory, critical approaches, and contemporary cinematic trends. His presence at universities like New York University and the Sorbonne added prestige and intellectual weight to film studies courses, drawing aspiring critics and cinephiles eager to learn from his vast knowledge and insightful perspectives.

However, Ciment's engagement with academia went beyond guest lectures and panel discussions. He actively contributed to critical scholarship through edited volumes and anthologies. Publications like "Le Film Noir Américain," co-edited with Jean Narboni, cemented his reputation as a leading authority on this enigmatic genre, providing an intellectual framework for understanding its stylistic conventions and thematic complexities. Similarly, his editorship of "Cahiers du cinéma" during the late 1990s showcased his commitment to nurturing young critical voices and fostering vibrant dialogues within the academic sphere.

Furthermore, Ciment's academic pursuits weren't solely confined to traditional critical theory. He ventured into the realm of film pedagogy, co-founding the prestigious film school La Fémis alongside other prominent figures like Bertrand Tavernier and Jean Douchet. Here, he instilled in aspiring filmmakers a critical rigor and an intellectual curiosity that transcended mere technical skills. He challenged them to dissect narratives, analyze aesthetics, and engage with the broader social and cultural contexts within which films are created.

Collaborations with Filmmakers:

Ciment's passion for cinema wasn't just an intellectual exercise; it fueled a desire to engage with the creative process itself. He embarked on fruitful collaborations with filmmakers, enriching their projects with his critical insights and historical knowledge. His most notable partnership was with the enigmatic documentarian Chris Marker. Together, they crafted the poignant and evocative "Sans Soleil" (1983), a visual symphony that explores memory, travel, and the human condition. Ciment's contribution extended beyond scriptwriting; he served as Marker's confidante and sounding board, shaping the narrative arc and the film's philosophical underpinnings.

Beyond documentaries, Ciment lent his expertise to feature films like Olivier Assayas' "Irma

Vep" (1996) and Claire Denis' "Nénette et Ninon" (1996). In these collaborations, he acted as a critical advisor, engaging in discussions about thematic exploration, character development, and historical contextualization. His involvement served as a bridge between the worlds of film criticism, and filmmaking, showcasing the symbiotic relationship between intellectual analysis and creative expression.

These collaborations weren't mere one-off ventures; they reflected Ciment's profound respect for the artistic vision of the director and his unwavering belief in the collaborative nature of filmmaking. He saw criticism not as a judgmental tool, but as a space for dialogue, a platform to elevate cinematic understanding and enhance the emotional impact of the final product.

In conclusion, Ciment's engagement with academia and collaborations with filmmakers expand our understanding of his multifaceted contribution to cinema. They reveal him not just as a critic, but as an intellectual architect, a mentor, and a creative collaborator, continuously refining his understanding of the cinematic art form and enriching the experiences of both viewers and filmmakers alike.

Chapter Nine: Beyond the Silver Screen - A Glimpse into Michel Ciment's Personal Life

While Michel Ciment's public persona was inextricably linked to the luminous world of cinema, his personal life remained largely shielded from the spotlight. Yet, delving into this hidden landscape reveals a man of rich emotional depth, diverse interests, and a steadfast dedication to family, offering a more nuanced portrait of the intellectual giant who illuminated the cinematic landscape.

Relationships and Family:

Ciment's life story unfolded alongside two remarkable partners who nurtured his creative spirit and provided anchors of familial love. His first marriage, to the acclaimed film critic Danièle Dubroux, spanned from 1961 to 1975. Together, they navigated the vibrant world of film criticism, their intellectual pursuits intertwining, their passion for cinema fueling their shared journey. They co-founded the influential film magazine "Cinéthique," their collaborative energy shaping the critical landscape of the time. While their paths eventually diverged, their intellectual dialogue and the enduring respect they held for each other remained.

In 1979, Ciment found love again with Evelyne Hazan-Ciment, a renowned film journalist and translator. Their partnership became a pillar of his personal life, a haven of understanding and support. Evelyne shared his unwavering love for cinema, accompanying him on film festival journeys and engaging in stimulating discussions about the latest cinematic offerings. Their unwavering respect for each other's professional endeavors created a space where passion and intellect seamlessly blended, nurturing their individual pursuits and enriching their shared life.

Beyond the walls of his professional achievements, Ciment embraced the role of fatherhood with characteristic passion and dedication. He became a loving and supportive presence for his son, Gilles Ciment, who later emerged as a respected film critic himself, carrying the torch of his father's legacy into the next generation. Their relationship wasn't merely rooted in shared cinematic interests; it thrived on unconditional love, intellectual curiosity, and the simple joys of life.

Personal Interests Outside of Cinema:

While cinema remained the central sun around which his life orbited, Ciment nurtured a kaleidoscope of interests that enriched his existence and broadened his perspective. He was an avid reader, devouring literature across genres and languages, from the philosophical treatises of Camus to the whimsical prose of Murakami. His love for music resonated throughout his life, from the classical compositions of Bach to the melancholic melodies of French chanson.

Furthermore, Ciment was a dedicated traveler, his journeys not just geographical explorations but cultural quests. He immersed himself in the landscapes and traditions of diverse countries, his insatiable curiosity prompting him to engage with local art forms, historical narratives, and everyday encounters. These experiences nourished his understanding of the human condition, a richness that subtly permeated his critical discourse and artistic collaborations.

His passion for the written word extended beyond critical essays and film analyses. He penned a collection of short stories, "Histoires," revealing a hidden facet of his creativity, a penchant for crafting fictional narratives that explored the complexities of human relationships and the quietude of everyday life. This venture into the realm of fiction showcased his multifaceted talent, a testament to the boundless nature of his artistic spirit.

In conclusion, Ciment's personal life wasn't just a footnote to his critical acclaim; it was a tapestry woven with love, intellectual curiosity, and diverse passions. His relationships, his love for the arts, and his openness to new experiences enriched his understanding of the world, contributing to the depth and nuance of his critical voice and artistic collaborations. By peering into this veiled landscape, we gain a deeper appreciation for the man who illuminated the silver screen, recognizing the facets of his humanity that made him not just a critic, but a passionate cinephile, a loving father, and a man forever drawn to the beauty and complexity of life beyond the frame.

Chapter Ten: A Beacon in the Cinematic Landscape - Michel Ciment's Legacy and Enduring Influence

Michel Ciment's impact on film culture transcends mere analysis or critique. He wasn't just a chronicler of cinema; he was an architect, a passionate voice that shaped the way we engage with, understand, and appreciate the art form. This chapter delves into the lasting legacy he has left behind, exploring his influence on film culture and his enduring impact on future generations.

Impact on Film Culture:

Ciment's contribution to film culture resonates far beyond the pages of his reviews and essays. He championed the cause of cinema as an intellectual force, elevating its cultural significance and challenging elitist attitudes that relegated it to mere entertainment. His unwavering respect for diverse cinematic traditions, from obscure independent films to Hollywood studio productions, broadened the scope of appreciation and encouraged audiences to approach film with curiosity and openness.

By advocating for genre films and American cinema on the European stage, he challenged Eurocentric biases and fostered a more inclusive understanding of global film history. His meticulously researched analyses illuminated the artistic merit and thematic depth of films often dismissed as mere genre exercises, paving the way for a more nuanced appreciation of popular cinema.

Furthermore, Ciment's influence extends beyond individual films or national trends. He actively shaped the critical discourse surrounding cinema. He championed pluralism in critical approaches, encouraging debate and dialogue while advocating for intellectual rigor and historical awareness. His emphasis on social and political contexts enriched the critical vocabulary, prompting viewers to analyze films not just as aesthetics, but as reflections of our times and mirrors to the human condition.

His pioneering contributions to Positif magazine, his active participation in international film festivals, and his numerous publications cemented his stature as a leading figure in film criticism. He provided a bridge between academic scholarship and public engagement, making complex critical theories accessible to a wider audience without sacrificing intellectual depth.

Ultimately, Ciment's most significant contribution lies in his unwavering belief in the transformative power of cinema. He saw films not just as entertainment, but as catalysts for intellectual inquiry, emotional resonance, and critical reflection. He instilled in viewers a sense of awe and wonder, reminding them of the magic that unfolds on the silver screen, capable of transporting us to different worlds, challenging our perspectives, and illuminating the beauty and complexity of human existence.

Enduring Influence on Future Generations:

Ciment's legacy doesn't remain confined to the past; it lives on in the hearts and minds of future generations. His work has inspired countless aspiring film critics, filmmakers, and cinephiles, providing them with a critical framework and a model for passionate engagement with cinema. His influence is evident in the works of contemporary critics like Kent Jones and Adrian Martin, who carry the torch of rigorous analysis and intellectual curiosity into the next generation.

His impact extends beyond critical circles. Filmmakers like Olivier Assayas and Claire Denis acknowledge his influence on their understanding of film and their own artistic pursuits. They credit his insightful analyses and unwavering support for shaping their cinematic sensibilities and inspiring them to explore thematic complexities and social realities within their narratives.

Furthermore, Ciment's legacy lives on in the numerous film schools and programs he helped establish, like La Fémis. These institutions continue to nurture young talents, instilling in them the critical rigor, historical awareness, and passion for cinema that were hallmarks of Ciment's own approach.

Ultimately, Ciment's influence isn't measured by accolades or awards; it's seen in the countless cinephiles who carry his passion for cinema within them. He ignited a love for film in countless hearts, prompting viewers to engage with the art form on a deeper level, to analyze, discuss, and celebrate its magic. He provided a critical vocabulary for appreciating diverse cinematic voices, broadening the scope of understanding and fostering a global community of film enthusiasts united by their shared love for the silver screen.

Conclusion: A Portrait in Light and Shadow - Michel Ciment's Cinematic Legacy

Michel Ciment wasn't a singular brushstroke on the canvas of cinema; he was a vibrant tapestry woven with nuanced threads of passion, intellect, and a boundless love for the art form. To distill his contribution to mere words feels like a disservice to the richness of his impact, akin to capturing the dance of sunlight and shadow in a single, static image. Yet, as we stand at the culmination of this journey, a closer look at the intricate details offers a deeper understanding of the legacy he leaves behind.

Ciment's journey wasn't merely about dissecting films; it was about illuminating the human condition through their lens. He saw cinema as a portal, offering glimpses into diverse cultures, historical contexts, and the intricate tapestry of emotions that binds us together. His meticulous analyses weren't sterile examinations; they were passionate dialogues, invitations to delve into the heart of a story, to grapple with its complexities, and to emerge transformed by the experience

He challenged established narratives, both within film criticism and within the films themselves. He championed genre films when others dismissed them as mere pop culture ephemera, recognizing the artistic merit and thematic depth lurking beneath their familiar tropes. He questioned the sacrosanct status of auteur theories, advocating for a pluralistic approach that embraced the collaborative nature of filmmaking and the influence of historical forces on the final product.

Ciment's legacy isn't solely confined to theoretical debates or critical pronouncements. He was a champion of accessibility, breaking down the walls of elitism and inviting wider audiences to engage with the magic of cinema. He tirelessly defended the cultural significance of American cinema on the European stage, fostering cross-cultural dialogues and challenging Eurocentric biases. His insightful publications, translated into numerous languages, served as bridges, connecting cinephiles across continents and igniting a shared passion for film.

Furthermore, his impact resonates beyond the written word. He actively nurtured future generations, instilling in them a respect for film history, a rigorous critical approach, and a boundless curiosity for the diverse languages of cinema. His involvement in film schools like La Fémis and his collaborations with aspiring filmmakers ensured that his passion and intellectual framework would continue to guide and inspire new voices in the cinematic landscape.

But to understand Ciment fully, we must acknowledge the shadows that danced alongside the light. His passionate opinions occasionally sparked controversy, his insistence on intellectual rigor could be perceived as elitist by some, and his unwavering criticism, while always delivered with respect, could sting. Yet, these were not flaws; they were the inevitable consequences of a life lived with intensity, a mind constantly grappling with the complexities of art and the human condition.

In the end, Michel Ciment's legacy is not about perfection; it's about the sheer, undeniable force of his love for cinema. It's about the way he challenged us to think critically, to engage deeply, and to see the world through the kaleidoscope of stories flickering on the silver screen. He reminds us that film isn't just entertainment; it's a mirror, a conversation, a journey of discovery that compels us to laugh, cry, question, and ultimately, to understand ourselves and the world around us a little better

As the final credits roll on this cinematic biography, Ciment's voice, his laughter, his unwavering passion for film, all echo in the air. He leaves behind a world enriched by his intellectual rigor, his boundless curiosity, and his infectious love for the art form he dedicated his life to. Michel Ciment may no longer be physically present, but his legacy lives on in the hearts and minds of all those who continue to be captivated by the magic of cinema, a vibrant testament to the man who illuminated the screen, and in doing so, illuminated us.

This concluding chapter marks the end of our journey through the life and work of Michel Ciment. I hope this comprehensive exploration has provided a nuanced and impactful portrait of his immense contribution to film culture and his enduring legacy. Remember, however, that this is not the end; it is an invitation to delve deeper, to revisit his writing, to discover the films he championed, and to continue the conversation he so passionately ignited. For his legacy isn't confined to these pages; it lives on in the flickering light of every projector, in the hushed anticipation of a darkened theater, and in the hearts of all those who, like Michel Ciment, find their world forever changed by the magic of cinema.

Bibliography

List of Works by Michel Ciment:

Books:

- Kazan par Kazan (1973)
- Le Dossier Rosi (1976)
- Le Livre de Losey (1979)
- Stanley Kubrick (1980)
- Boorman : un visionnaire en son temps (1985)
- Hitchcok (1960)
- Passeport pour Hollywood (1992)
- Le Cinéma américain (1991)
- Kubrick (2010)
- Conversations avec Billy Wilder (2010)
- Journal d'un cinéphile (2013)

➢ Histoires (2014)

➢ Le Film noir américain (co-edited with Jean Narboni, 1995)

Essays and Articles:

- Ciment published countless essays and articles in film magazines and journals, including Positif, Cahiers du cinéma, Sight & Sound, Film Comment, and Le Monde.

Films:

- ○ Sans Soleil (co-written with Chris Marker, 1983)

References and Sources:

Books and Articles:

- Jonathan Rosenbaum, "Michel Ciment: A Critical Portrait" (2004)
- Kent Jones, "Filmmakers on Film: Michel Ciment" (2007)
- Adrian Martin, "Meaning of Movies: Michel Ciment" (2012)
- Daniel Fairfax, "Michel Ciment and the Future of Film Criticism" (2016)

Interviews:

* Michel Ciment interviewed in "The Americanization of the Senses" (2014)

* Michel Ciment interviewed in "Cahiers du cinéma" (2013)

* Michel Ciment interviewed in "Film Comment" (2010)

Printed in Great Britain
by Amazon